NUEVO CALIFORNIA

Bernardo Solano & Allan Havis

based on material researched and developed by Bernardo Solano

BROADWAY PLAY PUBLISHING INC
56 E 81st St., NY NY 10028-0202
212 772-8334 fax: 212 772-8358
http://www.BroadwayPlayPubl.com

NUEVO CALIFORNIA
© Copyright 2005 by Bernardo Solano & Allan Havis

First printing: January 2005
I S B N: 0-88145-251-3

Book design: Marie Donovan
Word processing: Microsoft Word
Typographic controls: Xerox Ventura Publisher 2.0 P E
Typeface: Palatino
Printed and bound in the U S A

ABOUT THE AUTHORS

Bernardo Solano: A graduate of the Yale School of Drama, Mr Solano is the recipient of a 2001-03 N E A / T C G Theater Residency Program for Playwrights, Fulbright and McKnight Fellowships, N E A and Rockefeller grants, as well as an A T & T OnStage and two Lila Wallace-Reader's Digest grants. His work has been produced at San Diego Repertory Theater, Cornerstone Theater, Cincinnati Playhouse in the Park, George Street Playhouse, Naked Angels, INTAR Theater, Mixed Blood Theater, Borderlands Theater, L A Opera, and Mark Taper Forum's New Work Festival. In film and television: for P B S, U S A Network, Paramount and Universal Studios. Mr Solano is on the faculty at California State Polytechnic University, Pomona. NUEVO CALIFORNIA was named Outstanding New Play of the 2002-03 season by the San Diego Critics Circle.

Allan Havis: His plays have been produced by San
Diego Rep, Malashock Dance/Old Globe, Seattle's
A C T, Mixed Blood, Long Wharf, L A's Odyssey,
Hartford Stage, American Repertory Theater, South
Coast Rep, Virginia Stage Company, Philadelphia
Theater Company, and Berkshire Theater Festival,
Ensemble Studio Theater, K P B S radio, and W P A.
Commissions from San Diego Rep, South Coast Rep,
National Foundation for Jewish Culture, England's
Chichester Festival, C S C Rep, Sundance, Mixed Blood,
Ted Danson's film company, Malashock Dance, and
the University of California. Ten full length plays have
been published, including a novel *Albert the Astronomer*
(Harper & Row). He has recently edited an anthology
American Political Plays for University of Illinois Press.
Fellowships from N E A, Guggenheim, Rockefeller,
McKnight. Awards from H B O, C B S, The Kennedy
Center and S D Drama Critics Circle. He heads the
M F A Playwriting program at U C San Diego and
holds an M F A from Yale.

NEUVO CALIFORNIA was originally commissioned and produced by San Diego Repertory Theater (Sam Woodhouse, Artistic Director; Karen Wood, Managing Director), opening on 1 February 2003. The cast and creative contributors were:

THE BIRD .... Dora Arreola
POPE FELIPE .... John Campion
SIN FIN .... Jennifer Chu
JAIME .... Fernando Flores Vega
FENCE VENDOR &
MAN STANDING STILL ... Mark Christopher Lawrence
DAVID ....Steve Lipinsky
MAGGIE ....Catalina Maynard
ALBERT .... Gino Montesino
JUANA .... Presa
REBECCA ....Sylvia M'Lafi Thompson

Director ....Sam Woodhouse
Choreographer .... Dora Arreola
Set & lighting design ....Trevor Norton
Costume design ....Melanie Watnick
Music curator .... Hans Fjellestad
Sound design ....George Ye
Production stage manager ....Dana V Anderson

CHARACTERS

To be played by an ensemble of 10 actors

CHORUS 1-8
POPE FELIPE
THE BIRD
FENCE VENDOR
JUANA SANCHEZ
REBECCA ROWLAND
BYSTANDER
MAGGIE FLACKETT
ALBERT VENADO
JAIME FERNANDEZ
SIN FIN
PRESIDENT MILLICENT GOLD
PRESIDENTE HECTOR CORTEZ
VALET
MOURNERS
DAVID LERMAN
MILITANT CHICANO
OLD HOMELESS MAN
THUGS
SOMALIAN BYSTANDER
PERUVIAN MAN
CAMPSEINA WOMAN
CHINESE WOMAN
UNIFIED PATROL OFFICER
SUBURBAN MAN
NEW CAL SUPPORTERS
MAN STANDING STILL

SETTING

Time: the year 2028

A stretch of unusual beach where Mexico meets the United States. A large steel fence cuts through the space like a fantastic knife.

Allan Havis dedicates this book to the memory Caitlin (Kate) Clark, a superlative actor

special thanks to Sam Woodhouse

special thanks from Bernard Solano to Paula, Raphael and Lena. And the hundreds of community members from San Diego, Tijuana and Mexicali who shared their vision of the region with us.

thanks to The James Irvine Foundation, The Animating Democracy Initiative—a program of Americans for the Arts—funded by the Ford Foundation, San Diego Commission for Arts and Culture, Fideicomiso—U S Mexico Fund for Culture, National Endowment for the Arts, Theater Communications Group, Metropolitan Life Foundation, and California Arts Council

ACT ONE

(Nortec music plays. Onstage is a portion of a ten-foot high solid-steel fence. The floor of the stage is covered with sand; formerly San Diego/Tijuana County, newly named Nuevo California. 2028. Lights come up on a CHORUS *of actors)*

CHORUS 1: In the year 2000, a U S border patrol officer said that the border fence between San Diego and Tijuana was built to stop drug smugglers and the loss of innocent lives.

CHORUS 2: A Mexican cab driver said that the fence at the border was built to protect Mexico from losing the rest of itself to the United States.

CHORUS 3: In 2007, a U S geologist said the border wall was built to address pressure differentials between the two countries.

CHORUS 4: A Mexican commuter wanted to know why sixteen people in sixteen lanes at the border could decide who entered the United States, when *pinche* Sea World has least thirty lanes.

CHORUS 5: In 2016, a Mexican journalist said "Americans buy more and have more—why should they share that?"

CHORUS 6: An American bus driver said "Mexicans have strong families, strong morals—why should they change that?"

CHORUS 7: And then, in the year 2023, the unthinkable happened. Like a thunderclap:

CHORUS 8: 8.7

CHORUS 2: The ground split open

CHORUS 5: Buildings collapsed

CHORUS 1: Bridges crumbled

CHORUS 3: Los Angeles disappeared

CHORUS 4: Swallowed by God

CHORUS 6: Felipe

CHORUS 8: The great Pope

CHORUS 7: U S citizen, born in Mexico

CHORUS 2: He came

CHORUS 3: He comforted

CHORUS 6: He convened

CHORUS 1: We rebuilt

CHORUS 4: San Diego

CHORUS 5: Rebuilt

CHORUS 8: Tijuana

CHORUS 7: We imagined a new world, a new community

CHORUS 2: And yet, now, in the year 2028

CHORUS 4: A Blind musician doesn't see it

CHORUS 6: But his eyes

CHORUS 1: Can feel the cold, hard steel of

ALL: A cyclone fence

(One of the CHORUS *begins singing a melancholy version of* Que Seas Feliz*)*

CHORUS/SINGER: *Que sean feliz,*
feliz, feliz
es todo lo que pido
en nuestra despedida.
No pudo ser
despues de haberles amado tanto,
por todas esas cosas
tan absurdas de la vida.

(During the song, each CHORUS *member slowly leaves the*
stage. We hear a strange whispering sound, then a BIRD—
up to now unseen by the audience—unfurls its wings,
revealing FELIPE, *asleep. The* BIRD *looks like it is about*
to devour FELIPE, *who suddenly awakes with a start.*
The BIRD *has disappeared.)*

FELIPE: *(To God)* Sweet Father... Why? Why do you send
me another terrifying dream of death, when I am so
close to a paradise on earth?

(Lights up on Playas. A multi-ethnic crowd carrying signs in
support of "Nuevo California" bursts onstage. The signs say:
"BRAVO NUEVO 2028!" "GOD BLESS NEW CAL"
"VIVA NUEVO CALIFORNIA" "NEW CAL '28!")

(DAVID LERMAN, an American carrying several cameras
and wearing press passes, takes photographs. The crowd
sings Tumbala.)

CROWD: *La barda caerá mañana!*
That means the wall will fall,
And tomorrow our dreams
Will see from here to there!
Sin frontera, fin de una era!

Tumbala, Tumbala
Make it tumble to the ground
Tumbala, tumbala
A rumble heard all around

Movement equals *libertad;*
Nuestras ideas and feelings freed.
Our two way ticket *de oportunidad*
Is north and south to *felicidad.*

Tumbala, Tumbala
Let us rejoice in the sound.
Tumbala, Tumbala
Let it tumble to the ground
Tumbala, tumbala
The Great Wall is gonna fall!

(A FENCE VENDOR *hawks small panels cut from the border fence to the audience)*

FENCE VENDOR: *(In street slang)* Welcome ta Nuevo California! Get um while I got em. Buy your own piece a da offensive defensive fence! Yeah, boy! I'm selling what's left of Gulf War Marsden Matting Solid Steel Planking, imported exclusively from da Kuwaiti "oasis" ta build da great border wall of 1992. *(Indicating the still-standing fence)* 'At's right, son! Yo daddy landed jets onis fence long before we beat da crap out of Iraq and turned Arabia into a big ole Jiffy Lube. So buy your own piece a dis marvelous offensive fence. It's the shizznit! Welcome ta Nuevo California! Yeah, son! *(In Russian)* Young lady! *(In German)* Welcome, *(In French)* enjoy your stay *(In Chinese)* in Nuevo California!

(Alone in her own picket line, JUANA SANCHEZ, *a young Mexican woman, carries a sign with Spanish writing on one side, English on the other, saying: "Devuelvase a Roma, Papa/Pope go back to Rome")*

JUANA: *Devuelvase a Roma, Papa!* Pope, go back to Rome!

FENCE VENDOR: *Señorita, le puedo interesar en—*

JUANA: *Largase!*

FENCE VENDOR: I'll give you da fly-babe discount, a'ight? *(She spits on the piece of fence in the* FENCE VENDOR'*s hand.)*

JUANA: *(To* FENCE VENDOR*) Que me importa, yo ya perdi todo.*

FENCE VENDOR: Yo, dat don't give you da right to spit at a brotha! Ole girl don't know a baller when she see one. *(Exiting, to audience)* Welcome ta Nuevo California! Buy your own piece of spectacular history...of memories and intimate happiness and shit!

(The FENCE VENDOR *exits in one direction,* JUANA *in another.)*

*(*REBECCA ROWLAND, *a forty-something African-American television journalist, is about to begin a live report.)*

REBECCA: Good evening, dear America young and old, this is Rebecca Rowland and I'm here live in Las Playas, where the infamous border fence meets the Pacific Ocean, a beautiful stretch of beach that straddles two countries. Just three miles west from Avenida Revolucion—the very center of old Tijuana...in the distance, a Mariachi band serenades rich gringos, as barmaids pour out ten thousand frosted margaritas. Were the stakes anything less, one would call this high comedy from the gods. *(Indicating fence)* The border fence...it divides the land like a knife, and even slices into the ocean. One year ago, U S Homeland Security patrolled these shores. But now the scene is thoroughly—

BYSTANDER: We love you, Rebecca!

REBECCA: Right back at you, sweet-pea. *(Indicating another part of fence)* The border. Profound or ludicrous? You decide. Tomorrow a small portion of this two-thousand mile fence will no longer stand. San Diego and Tijuana will become one—Nuevo California.

Conceived nearly five years ago in the rubble of the most terrifying earthquake in five hundred years. And of course mid-wifed by the first Mexican-American Pontiff: the youthful, unpredictable, charismatic Pope Felipe.

(*As* REBECCA *lets her last comment sink in,* DAVID *enters and watches her.*)

REBECCA: Feliz Filipe. Poet, philosopher, popular recording artist. Orphan of Mexico City, bred in Washington D C. The Pope's shrouded family lineage could not prevent his miraculous and meteoric rise. Nor could Nuevo California be born without him. Of course, Mexico's explosion of new oil certainly sweetened the deal. *(Beat)* New Cal, like a phoenix, rose from the ashes of Los Angeles and Orange County. This transformation was sparked by massive federal aid and matching grants from Taco Bell.

(DAVID *takes* REBECCA's *picture, she winks at him.*)

REBECCA: Tomorrow, Pope Felipe will preside at this very spot-despite weeks of muncipal building bombings, fires, and a sarin gas attack in the county court house. *(Beat)* So let's go back in time, if you will. 2003. Back when I was a novice journalist, a semi-virgin, and take out pizza was only eight ninety-nine. I asked some teenagers on both sides of the border how they felt about the fence between them:

(MAGGIE FLACKETT, JAIME FERNANDEZ *and* ALBERT VENADO *all appear, each isolated in light; they are all in their teens.*)

MAGGIE: I'm Maggie Flackett, in 2004 I'll be a senior at Madison High. Go War Hawks! Dude, everything is so corrupt down there. We need that Fence.

ALBERT: Okay. Albert Venado, almost twenty, I'm a Kumeyaay Indian. The border fence split the Kumeyaay nation in half.

JAIME: *Soy Jaime Fernandez, 17 anos, y soy un rebelde intelectual contra los imperialistas norte americanos.* You steal our food, our drinks, our music. And make us give el Mickey Mouse a blowjob.

MAGGIE: Mexican laws are so screwy! Except for their drinking age, that's a good one!

ALBERT: English one side, Spanish on the other. No room for our Kumeyaay tongue. I'll tell you this, my grandmother is one pissed off Indian.

(JAIME *hoots as his "sign-off".* MAGGIE, JAIME *and* ALBERT *disappear and we are back in the present with* REBECCA.)

REBECCA: Now, a full generation later as citizens of two countries surrender their respective National Library Cards, what are peoples' true sentiments about the fence coming down today?

(REBECCA *approaches Juana and her "Devuelvase a Roma, Papa/Go Back to Rome, Pope" sign)*

REBECCA: Excuse me, *señorita...*

JUANA: *NO HABLO INGLES.*

REBECCA: *No problemo.* Why do you want the Pope to go back to Rome?

JUANA: I do not want the Pope singing his fake songs in my city. *(She walks away.)*

REBECCA: Thank you, señorita. *(Back to audience/camera)* Indeed, this provocative Pope sings his *favorite* songs wherever he goes. For many years he was a conservative Vatican Cardinal, but in the last twelve months he has surprised the Catholic hierarchy with his startling progressive innovations. Some say there is Jewish blood in his veins, but they said the same about

Jesus. There's Albert Venado, tribal chairperson of the Kumeyaay Indians and Viejas power plant. Venado and Pope Felipe are cultural bedfellows, always sharing a bottle of fine scotch and Cuban cigars courtesy of Presidente Elian Gonzales.

(REBECCA *approaches Kumeyaay Indian* ALBERT VENADO, *now a middle-aged man.*)

REBECCA: Mr Venado, you and I have known each other for so many...

ALBERT: Sorry, I can't.

REBECCA: ...years. Rowland, I B C News...

ALBERT: No time.

(ALBERT *walks away. A* MILITANT CHICANO *enters, speaks to* REBECCA *and the cameras.*)

MILITANT CHICANO: Big day for the U S, Mexican relations and the hip Pope.

REBECCA: Sir, would you care to share your thoughts about Nuevo California?

MILITANT CHICANO: There's something that Chicanos never have, never will forget: we didn't cross the fucking border. *La frontera*...it *(Beep)* crossed us. *Viva la Raza.*

(*An* OLD HOMELESS MAN *has been listening.*)

OLD HOMELESS MAN: That's right, young blood. (*To* REBECCA) Let me tell you something, Miss Oprah Winfrey! In 1848, after we won a war against our Mexican neighbors, seventy-five thousand of them decided to stay on what was now Uncle Sam's land and become citizens. Now, I don't have a home no more, but I like to think that I could be as brave as those folks and stick it out.

MILITANT CHICANO: *Orale, ese!*

OLD HOMELESS MAN: *(To* REBECCA*)* You sure is pretty. Wanna see my thing?!

REBECCA: No! But thank you, darling. People obviously have a lot to say about Nuevo California.

*(*REBECCA *approaches* SIN FIN, *a young hybrid woman of multiple ethnicities.)*

REBECCA: Rebecca Rowland I B C news. What are your thoughts about the fence coming down?

SIN FIN: I say hooray—*ole, porque en Nuevo California* we don't fight war, we *lucha* peace, we contort and retort to all those *dizques* north and south *quien* doubt *nuestro* resolve to earn equal *pago* for work—economy not lobotomy for our *trabajadora!* Not no more are we the *fronterizo* people, *desde ahora somos fronterzeros*, that means no more *frontera pa'fuera* cause the border *frontera* is history, *mano!* The Pope is dope cause *el sabe que el* sand is shifting sifting lifting our *espiritus sanctus!* Take *el tiempo* to feel, *nunca do el conceal y siempre siempre siempre* be the real. *Paz,* out!

*(*SIN FIN *exits.)*

REBECCA: *(To camera, gentle mocking)* "*Asi es la vida* if dat's what you needa"—the new lingo of New Cal! Don't freak if your kids speak like this before the week is out. And we once worried about Ebonics. *(Smiles)* Back in a moment. *(She is off-air now.)* David "insta-matic" Lerman.

DAVID: Rebecca "watchdog" Rowland-who are you going to bury this week?

REBECCA: Only the people I truly love.

DAVID: You took down a Supreme Court Justice in less time than it takes me to take a tinkle.

REBECCA: A fish rots first at the head and works downward. Felipe said that to me when he gave me that exclusive. *(Crocodile charm)* You know I can get anyone to tell me anything.

DAVID: Is that how you got O J's deathbed confession?

REBECCA: That was easy, I dated his second cousin Melvin. *(Wink)* Sorry about your not getting the Pulitzer.

DAVID: Can you believe I got beat out by octogenarian Hilary Clinton on her sequel, IT TAKES A VILLAGE IDIOT.

REBECCA: *(Beat)* They're going to sabotage Nuevo California.

DAVID: Who?

REBECCA: The all white, circumcised militia.

DAVID: Oh?

REBECCA: Or maybe the Aryan Nation with jackboots and cute little armbands. You can guess along.

DAVID: I'm not a fortune teller, cupcake.

REBECCA: I like fortunetellers.

DAVID: I like cupcakes. Real enough to hold in my two hands. Tell the folks at the network I said hi.

REBECCA: Sure and tell the folks at the magazine they can kiss my tattooed ass.

DAVID: *(As he exits)* Which cheek? The one that says "Media Diva" or "Cassandra dearest"?

REBECCA: The left one, baby.

(REBECCA blows him a kiss and exits. Lights up on FELIPE blow-drying his hair. He turns on the T V as he opens a gift; a bottle of rare scotch.)

T V ANNOUNCER: *(V O)* The Presidents of Mexico and the U S met today at Camp David to prepare for the birth of Nuevo California while facing the ongoing

ACT ONE 11

crisis with Saudi Arabia's halted oil production. It was
also the occasion of President Millicent Gold's sixtieth
birthday. E S P N's cameras were there.

(We hear the voices of the two presidents.)

PRESIDENT GOLD: Tomorrow is a magical day for our
countries, Señor Presidente.

FELIPE: Idiot.

PRESIDENTE CORTEZ: Every day is momentous, as the
price of crude oil plummets, Madam President.

FELIPE: Imbecile.

PRESIDENT GOLD: OPEC owes Mexico a debt of
gratitude.

FELIPE: Moron.

PRESIDENTE CORTEZ: Nuevo California deserves to
inherit the last of the Earth's "black gold."

FELIPE: Half-wit.

PRESIDENT GOLD: I have fears about these dangerous
fringe elements, Presidente Cortez.

FELIPE: Pendeja.

PRESIDENTE CORTEZ: Yes, President Gold, on the left
and right.

FELIPE: Two jackasses.

PRESIDENTE CORTEZ/GOLD: *Salud*/Cheers.

FELIPE: May God relieve Himself in your best French
champagne. *(He turns off the T V.)* Fools, I've only just
begun.

(A knock on the door)

FELIPE: Pronto.

VOICE OF VALET: *(In Italian)* Your Eminence, Albert
Venado is here. *(In English)* He is on your calendar.

FELIPE: *(Aware his valet is upset about the bathrobe)*
Let Albert in. He's like a Son! Kiri Te Kanawa on.

(Kiri Te Kanawa music begins playing softly.)

(ALBERT enters.)

ALBERT: You've got a humungous, irate Cardinal just
in from Rome...

FELIPE: Yes...

ALBERT: ...who's beating a path into the hotel carpet.
He's incensed that I jumped ahead of him.

FELIPE: Another walrus in need of a pair of Nikes.
One hundred more laps.

*(FELIPE embraces ALBERT who recoils from a powerful odor
coming from FELIPE; he tries to cover his reaction to it.)*

ALBERT: I'm glad you asked me to come.

FELIPE: I'm glad you're sitting on a dozen oil wells.

ALBERT: Better wealthy than poor.

FELIPE: Better witty than a bore.

ALBERT: So honored to be on the review stand with you
tomorrow.

FELIPE: And I'm so sorry to hear about your
grandmother's passing.

ALBERT: *Gracias.*

FELIPE: May she rest in peace.

ALBERT: *(Beat)* Your Eminence, I need to talk to you
about the rise in terrorism here.

FELIPE: *(Lightly)* Let's have a drink. So tell me, Alberto,
am I to fear every malcontent? Or as you Kumeyaay
people say, *Ka Kwai Me Yo?*

ALBERT: You just asked me if your buttocks are firm.

FELIPE: Did I?

ALBERT: It's not too late, you know.

FELIPE: To firm up my buttocks?

ALBERT: To cancel your speech.

FELIPE: Oh, don't be ridiculous. *Nullius addictus iurare in verva magistri.*

ALBERT: Dear Pontiff...you are a major target.

FELIPE: Good.

ALBERT: Look at your recent behavior: going on M T V Live, the crazy incognito street walks, the recorded children songs, risqué D V Ds-this looks like...

FELIPE: Show business? *(Hands* ALBERT *a complimentary C D)* Here's my latest C D.

ALBERT: *(Reading the C D's label)* "With Love From Above...?"

FELIPE: Catchy, huh?
(Singing some stanzas from the one of the hit songs)
"So many stars in the galaxy
in this timeless wonderland
So many dear starfish in the sea
in this luminous...
(Smiles coyly) The philosopher Hegel wrote that a solitary man—inspired—can turn history in a snap of a finger.

ALBERT: Isn't it enough that you want all Catholic churches to distribute free condoms at the end of mass?

FELIPE: Free, not ribbed. I'm not insane, Albert. I see clearly now. Since the earthquake. I demand nations tax all corporations on their gross. Universal health care. H I V and famine conquered. Restore human rights from China to Paraguay. And halt the sales of these horrid little white statues of the Pope. *(Holding one little figurine)*

ALBERT: *(Amused)* Anything else?

FELIPE: Invite women...

ALBERT: *(Flip)*...and gays to the priesthood?

FELIPE: The latter has been in place for over a thousand years. The glorious hypocrisy, Albert. Priests should be free to have sex—responsibly. A little pleasure never hurt anyone.

ALBERT: *(Unsure of* FELIPE's *irony)* I never know when you're joking.

FELIPE: My nose twitches like a rabbit. *(Beat)*

ALBERT: Rebecca Rowland phoned today. Tracking a rumor that that the Vatican is about to vote on your mental health.

FELIPE: *(Indicating the Cardinal outside)* It's not a rumor. The Cardinals have awoken from their coma and want to censure me. But they know most Catholics are behind me...

ALBERT: Most Catholics don't echo the College of Cardinals.

FELIPE: Yes, but I think you have it backwards, *mi amigo.*

ALBERT: You serve no good if the Cardinals vote you down publicly.

FELIPE: That's why I avoid going back to Rome, though I miss the caneloni in wine sauce terribly! I'm sure my staff is all Vatican spies. Besides the Cardinals can't excommunicate a Pontiff. It's never been done.

ALBERT: Okay, in plain English: you're scaring the shit out of me.

FELIPE: The world's spinning out of control. God speaks to me.

ALBERT: *(Incredulous)* Felipe... Is it that you want to push the globe right out of the sky?

FELIPE: A beautiful image, querido amigo. I remember the day we met. Just after the quake, five years ago.

ALBERT: People thought you'd turn out like every Pontiff: implacable, biblically old, more morbid than a corpse.

FELIPE: *(Smiling)* Surprise, surprise.

ALBERT: But you were like a fire of illumination. I felt it when I pressed my lips to your hand.

FELIPE: Nyet. Nein. No. We clenched hands that day.

ALBERT: It was a kiss.

FELIPE: It was a handshake. Don't argue with the Pope.

(Both clearly have different memories of the moment.)

FELIPE: Anyway, I hated that imbecilic custom.

ALBERT: *(joking)* Afraid of herpes?

FELIPE: Popes have no diseases. Are you turning more conservative?

ALBERT: More fearful. Oil changes everything. When you go back to Rome, who will lead us?

FELIPE: *(Ironically)* The mayors of Tijuana and San Diego are capable enough. Flipping a coin for the first two years has a poetic touch to it, don't you think?

ALBERT: Interesting no one even considered a Kumeyaay as Governor of Nuevo California.

FELIPE: *(Teasing)* You mean, like yourself?

ALBERT: We were here before the Spanish.

FELIPE: Then have compassion for the trespasser. Half the world is trespassing.

ALBERT: *(Beat)* I've an awful premonition, your Eminence.

FELIPE: Albert, fear is the devil.

ALBERT: Please don't give your speech tomorrow.

FELIPE: Would you rather I just wave from the review stand?

ALBERT: Yes.

FELIPE: I'll cut the speech in half.

ALBERT: I don't want your blood on my hands.

(FELIPE gives a glass to ALBERT, toasting.)

FELIPE: To Nuevo California.

ALBERT: To impossible dreams. *(Facetiously)* Lincoln. Martin Luther King. Pope Felipe.

FELIPE: God's angels will be with us tomorrow.

ALBERT: And the day after tomorrow? *(He exits.)*

FELIPE: Querido Padre...I can smell his fear.

(The beach at Playas. Music starts playing as a procession of "MOURNERS" enters with lit candles and offerings, JUANA among them. They sing "La Llorana". DAVID is nearby, taking photographs of them.)

MOURNERS: *Todos me dicen el negro llorona,*
Negro pero cariñoso.
Yo soy como el chile verde llorona,
Picante pero sabroso yo.

Ay de mi, llorona,
Llorona de ayer y hoy.
Ayer era maravilla, llorana,
Y ahora ni sombra soy.

(FELIPE, in disguise, enters and follows closely behind the MOURNERS.)

Dicen que no tengoo duelo, llorona,
Porque no me ven llorar.
Hay muertos que no hacen ruido, llorona,
Y es mas grande su penar.

(DAVID *catches a police detective's attention. The detective is*
the audience. DAVID *uses pantomime and the few words he*
knows in Spanish to make himself understood)

DAVID: Good evening...detective...no, *muy poco* Spanish.
I'm a photojournalist. I work for-sure, I D. David
Lerman. I understand this is some "Day of the Dead"
ceremony—at this time of year? ...No, kidding, they
think they're going to raise the spirits of people who've
died at the border? ...No, I'm just here to take pictures
of New Cal *(Beat)* I've noticed that security—*seguridad*—
for the Pope's appearance kinda sucks. *Muy malo.* Okay,
detective, I'll be *mucho cuidado.*

(DAVID *puts some distance between them; he notices* JUANA,
starts to take her photo.)

JUANA: *Quien le dio permiso de tomar mi foto?*

DAVID: Excuse me?

JUANA: *Mi foto.*

DAVID: Oh! Your photo. Would you like me to send it
to you?

JUANA: *Es usted del estado?*

DAVID: Actually I'm originally from Spain. An
inquisition made my Jewish family "emigrate."

JUANA: *No le entendio.*

DAVID: No, I don't play Nintendo. *(Holding out his hand,*
British accent) My name is Bond. James Bond. *(Smiles)*
David. Lerman.

JUANA: *¿No quiero que me tome la foto, me entiende?*

DAVID: No photo, sure...You should be flattered, you're pretty—*muy boniter*

JUANA: *Usted no tiene ni la menor idea de lo que le estoy diciendo. Usted es un tarado.*

DAVID: *(Laughing)* Oh! *¡Tarado! (Stops abruptly)* That wasn't a joke, was it? *(Beat)* Have I offended you?

JUANA: *Señor Lerman...los Estados Unidos me ofenden.*

ALBERT: *(Calling to* DAVID*) Pendejo.*

DAVID: *(Smiles, unawareof the insult) Pendejo.*

ALBERT: A little cultural slumming?

*(*DAVID *smiles diplomatically)*

ALBERT: Picture this. In the days of the Kumeyaay, when someone died, we'd remove the person's memories from the world. That way there'd be no reason for the dead guy to stay. So we would dig a pit and burn the dead's belongings...sing a song... and that'd release the memories of the deceased. *(Beat)* Let me know when you get that one developed.

MOURNERS: *Si al cielo subir pudiera, llorona,*
Las estrellas te bajara.
La luna a tus pies pusiera, llorona,
Con el sol te coronará.
Ay de me, llorona,
Llorona de negros ojos.
Ya con esta se despide, llorona,
Tu negrito soñador.

(The MOURNERS'*s song ends and they exit.* JUANA *is clearly disappointed that no spirits have shown up; she sees* ALBERT *and gives both him and* DAVID *the cold shoulder.* DAVID *and* ALBERT *consider each other for a moment, exit in opposite directions.* FELIPE, *nearby, hears the same soft whispering as from his dream, except now it becomes a murmur of many*

languages, crashing against each other, rendering them unintelligible)

FELIPE: What in God's name...

(Trying to locate the sound's origin, FELIPE *steps out a few feet into the "water." The whispering immediately stops. He notices* JUANA *standing at the edge of the beach)*

FELIPE: Did you hear that?

JUANA: *¿Perdon?*

FELIPE: It sounded like someone crying.

JUANA: *(Indicating the ocean) Es el mar.*

*(*JUANA *doesn't recognize* FELIPE, *but she too detects the unpleasant odor.)*

FELIPE: *Si*, a terrible odor. Wherever I go. There must be a sewage problem. *¿Usted es Mexicana?*

JUANA: *¿Si. Usted?*

FELIPE: I was raised in the U S, yes.

JUANA: *(Confirming her suspicion) Pocho. ¿Que edad?*

FELIPE: I was nine years old. I crossed the border—alone.

JUANA: *Pero usted se salvo. Muchos niños mueren. Por nada.*

FELIPE: Yes, I survived. But the children who've died because of this cursed fence...they will not be forgotten. This fence will go.

JUANA: The children become martyrs? *Es ridiculo.*

FELIPE: Not martyrs. *Corderos.* Lambs. Innocent victims. Of inequality.

JUANA: *(Agreeing) Si, pero...no es justo.*

FELIPE: You're right. Children shouldn't die for the sins of the adult—if you only read the scriptures, you miss the real life before your eyes.

(JUANA *offers* FELIPE *her scarf for his feet.*)

JUANA: *Tenga. Para sus pies.*

FELIPE: It's okay, it's just a little sand.

(JUANA *kneels and dries* FELIPE'S *feet.*)

FELIPE: *Gracias.*

JUANA: *La gente esta muy...*people very strange tonight. Mean people. Be careful, *señor.*

(JUANA *exits.* FELIPE *speaks to God.*)

FELIPE: Albert was terribly wrong.

(Further down along the beach, SIN FIN *is shouting to whoever will listen.)*

SIN FIN: Gentepeople! The land and sand of New Cal are the geography of the *almasoul, simbolo* of what's underneath the color of our skin, not *encima* the *clima.*

*(*FELIPE *observes from a distance as several anonymous* THUGS *approach* SIN FIN.*)*

THUG 1: If it ain't our favorite mongrel bitch.

SIN FIN: Gentepeople, *escuchan mi voz!* I am Sin Fin! Downsouth they call me baja-bigmouth!

THUG 2: You better shut that mouth now!

SIN FIN: Hear my call—*la* old order's gonna fall!

THUG 3: The only thing gonna fall is you.

(They begin to beat SIN FIN.*)*

SIN FIN: No, don't...*por favor...no dolor...no mas,* Tomás...

FELIPE: What...? Stop that! I said, stop it!

(They easily push FELIPE *aside.)*

THUG 1: *(To* SIN FIN*)* We know where you sleep!

THUG 2: And keep that pretty little hole shut!

THUG 3: Or we'll cut it off your face!

(The THUGS *exit.* FELIPE *runs to her side.)*

FELIPE: Are you all right?

SIN FIN: I would be dead she said!

FELIPE: Do you need a doctor?

SIN FIN: You my guardian angel, *doctor protector*?!

FELIPE: They tried to silence your beautiful words.
I'm sorry.

SIN FIN: Assault not your fault, *no su culpa, no disculpa!*

FELIPE: Are they coming back?

SIN FIN: *No sé*, can't say!

FELIPE: Do you know them?

SIN FIN: No, but they know me, *sepan* where I live,
pueden come back, slit my rack!

FELIPE: I'll take you to the police.

SIN FIN: No times ten!

FELIPE: I promise you safety.
(Begins to sing)
"So many stars in the galaxy
in this timeless wonderland.
So many dear starfish in the sea
in this luminous wonderland.
So many handsome souls in the tree
in this joyous wonderland."

SIN FIN: *Espera consejera.* The sound of your *voz veloz*
I've heard before *aqui en mi* core.

FELIPE: Just another wandering soul with dirty feet.

SIN FIN: I got voice solo *por usted*, Fred. You sound like
the sea at dusk. Like *la luna*, here to wash *mi alma* and
leave it *calma.*

FELIPE: *(Pointing to her mouth)* Poetry.

SIN FIN: *(Beat)* Come to see the fence set free *mananaday?*

FELIPE: I'm here to see.

SIN FIN: You speak *mi idioma, paloma.* Like the Pope, the hombre who wants what I want. *(Beat)* Gotta get away from this night full of fright. *Tengo que irme, firme.*

(SIN FIN exits. FELIPE hears the sound of flapping wings, but there's no bird to be seen. FELIPE takes off his disguise as music takes us into the next morning and he begins the ritual of dressing himself in his finest vestments. Playas. REBECCA enters, addresses the camera/audience)

REBECCA: Good morning, young America, dear America. It's *(date of presentation)*, 2028. Minutes away from the Pope's arrival here at Playas. Citizens, Las Vegas celebrities, world governments—all here with Rowland. *(Beat)* Yet our two nations' leaders are absent. Their handlers have cited bomb threats to both Presidents. But in truth, let's blame Gold and Cortez for pocketing muchos pesos. But I'm here and I've been asking folks about "Tumbala!" the fence coming down today.

(JAIME, the Tijuana teenager from 2003, now middle-aged, appears before REBECCA's cameras.)

JAIME: Jaime Fernandez, born here in T J—I'm sorry, "old Tijuana." Happy to own a trucking business, two taxi companies, and four mid-sized hotels. My employees are from all over the world. If they are willing to work, this Mexicano is willing to give them a chance. Go knock on Uncle Sam's door, he'll piss in your face.

REBECCA: Sir, I'm curious, if your daughter wanted to marry a *North* American, what advice would you give her?

JAIME: Get a second opinion. Long live Felipe.

(Playas. ALBERT *joins* FELIPE *as he says his prayers before greeting the multitude.)*

ALBERT: Did you know I was groomed to be a Kumeyaay healer?

(Pope nods)

ALBERT: Grandmother taught me the songs. One was about a monster that was devouring our children.

FELIPE: A brave boy tricks the monster and kills it.

ALBERT: Yes, so the boy becomes the tribal hero. Of course the kid dies, too.

FELIPE: Of course.

ALBERT: I stopped singing all our songs the day I realized that boy was a sacrificial lamb. That little boy is dead. *(Beat)* Felipe. The people on the street think that unifying Americans and Mexicans is....

FELIPE: We've seen what separation brings.

ALBERT: Can't you smell that odor? It's driving me insane.

FELIPE: Then cut off your nose. I cherish you, Alberto. More than you realize. There's something magical about our connection. How old was I when I escaped from the orphanage?

ALBERT: Nine. On foot, crossing the desert, a hundred miles east of Mexicali.

FELIPE: Yes. A torrential flood struck the ravine I was in...my death in a matter of seconds. There was a blinding light, then the glow of a supernatural hand.

ALBERT: God's hand?

FELIPE: I was fated to die as a boy. The signs were unmistakable.

ALBERT: Obviously God didn't agree.

FELIPE: I was *this* close to seeing His face.*(Beat)*
Either Christ or Satan deigned to extend my life.

ALBERT: Had to be Christ.

FELIPE: To this day I am unsure.

ALBERT: You work for Christ, it says so in all the major
guidebooks.

FELIPE: There was a time when Lucifer, of all the angels,
was favored by God. *(Beat)* There I was, expecting
death when suddenly a giant bird appeared.

ALBERT: Don't birds represent the Holy Spirit?

FELIPE: I made a pact with the bird and the vibrant,
giant hand lifted me high into the sky.

ALBERT: That must've been some pact.

FELIPE: Forget this nonsense. It was all a hallucination.

*(*MAGGIE, *the teenager from 2003, now a well-dressed
woman, appears with* REBECCA.*)*

MAGGIE: My name is Maggie Flackett, former
councilwoman from Fallbrook. *(Beat)* You know,
there's a saying from Robert Frost, "Good fences make
good neighbors." *(Pulling out a card)* The poem is
"Mending Wall." "to know what I was walling in..."

REBECCA: "...or walling out."

MAGGIE: Right. Art, like good sex, is in the eye of the
beholder. I moved to San Jose.

(Back to FELIPE *and* ALBERT*)*

FELIPE: Today...*will* be a great day. *(Lightening)* Did you
bring the Cuban cigars?

ALBERT: I know about the death threats.

FELIPE: So what if the "Nuevo" rich are afraid of Nuevo California.

ALBERT: Italo Calvino wrote about a bright city by the water.

FELIPE: Ah yes, clever Calvino.

ALBERT: Everything in the city has a mirror image, every action great and small duplicated, the one city that's reflected in the water reflects a twin city. So no one dares to take chances. The two cities live for each other, with no love between them, and no joy in tomorrow.

FELIPE: So?

ALBERT: So?

FELIPE: So I don't believe Calvino ever visited Nuevo California. How do I look?

ALBERT: Like a peacock.

FELIPE: "I'm ready for my fanfare, Mr Venado."

(Music signals the arrival of FELIPE*)*

REBECCA: This is it. The moment we've all been waiting for. Pope Felipe is approaching Playas.

(We become aware of JUANA, DAVID *and* ALBERT *among the crowd...*
DAVID *is taking photographs...*
JUANA *is a bundle of nervous energy...*
ALBERT *is concerned, constantly checking his watch...*
FELIPE *appears amidst the roar of the crowd. Inexplicable shadows hover around him.)*

FELIPE: So many kind faces among the unique. It does my heart good. *(Beat)* God smiles down upon us all. *(Beat)* I stand before this bit of rusted steel between two nations. These builders meant well, but it became a symbol of desperation. Some say this wall protects and preserves the people. I say this wall proclaims, "You have no place at your brother's table." I repeat, "...NO PLACE AT YOUR BROTHER'S TABLE." I know, as I too have been excluded. *(Beat)* Nuevo California. Say it the other way. California Nuevo. Is it impossible? I say it is forever possible. Water into wine. Loaves of bread and fish into a great banquet. We can live together not as an imperfect reflection, but as true equals— even true lovers. I offer you my hand.

(He notices the shadow of a bird hovering high above. He continues...)

FELIPE: Let us step forward, Let us greet the mysterious. Let us take a leap of faith. God's wonderous hand descends. Let us not be afraid.

(We see the glint of something shining in the sun....)

FELIPE: Let the walls come down! Let us not be afraid! Let the walls come—

(There is a loud and sudden gunshot...
FELIPE *clutches his chest and crumbles to the ground...*
Reality shifts as we see:
FELIPE *shot over and over again...*
Total pandemonium as ALBERT, JAIME, MAGGIE, JUANA *and* REBECCA *speaking the text below simultaneously...)*

REBECCA: Oh God!

JAIME: *¡Por el amor de Dios! ¿Quien hizo esto?!*

ALBERT: Dear God! Felipe! Please! Someone help! Please help!

JUANA: *No puede ser?! Como pudo pasar esto? Dios Mio!*

MAGGIE: Oh, God! Oh, God!

DAVID: Christ! Somebody shot the Pope!

(The whispering in many languages returns, but this time the sound is deafening. Blackout. Lights up, a short time later... REBECCA *is on-air.)*

REBECCA: *(Extremely upset, in mid-speech)* Rowland here. It's...it's been thirty minutes since the Holy Father was shot. I'm sorry. Very confusing here at Playas...the entire area has been sealed. The shooter has not been found. No eyewitnesses. Hundreds detained and questioned. Theories are cropping up about the C I A's complicity in the attack. One rumor links this action to extreme Vatican officials, another rumor to a powerful Tijuana drug ring linked to Mexico's ruling party. More to the point, why the hell was this not prevented? Why, I ask? Why? WHY?

*(*REBECCA *exits.* DAVID *joins a line of very upset and angry people waiting to be interviewed by the authorities. We see people leave the line and sit in front of the audience as if they are sitting before a detective and answering questions. A* SOMALIAN BYSTANDER *shoves* DAVID *from behind.)*

SOMALIAN BYSTANDER: *Gudub, gudub, gudub!* Move it!

DAVID: Hey, look, I know you're—

SOMALIAN BYSTANDER: *Haddii uu dhinto, waxaa dhacaysa dhibaato!* If he dies, there will be trouble!

DAVID: Anybody understand what this man is saying?!

SOMALIAN BYSTANDER: *(In English)* Fuck you!

DAVID: I understood that.

(Lights up on MAGGIE *being interviewed by detectives.)*

MAGGIE: Detectives, I'm sick about this...a man of God. ...Oh, your partner doesn't speak English. Well, okay...my nombre es Margaret Flackett. ...No, sir, I was looking at el Papa when the gun went off. *(To other detective)* What if I organized a rally—I've a constitutional right. Look, that doesn't mean I have it out for those people-I mean...I'm upset like everybody else. I think it an act of terrorism brought about by agents of-I can go now?

(Lights up on the line of people. DAVID *sees* JUANA *in the same line.)*

DAVID: *(To* JUANA*)* Sorry to have to meet again like this, I mean...are you okay?

(Off her look)

DAVID: Did you *(Pointing to his eye)* see anything?

JUANA: *No. Nada. ¿Y usted?*

DAVID: Busy taking pictures...

JUANA: *Hay gente diciendo que el Papa ha muerto.* Dead.

DAVID: He'll be okay. They'll give him new lungs, new heart, whatever it takes.

JUANA: *La muerte le puede venir a cualquiera.*

DAVID: You know, he kind of looks a little like my father. Black penetrating eyes floating over that eagle's beak. *(Beat)* He's going to be fine. I sense it. Really.

JUANA: *Dicho como un gringo.*

DAVID: That sounded like a racist remark.

JUANA: *¿¡Racista, yo?! Porque estas*—why are you here?!

*(*DAVID *draws a line in the sand between them.)*

DAVID: I want to see, okay?!

JUANA: *Ver que?!*

(He violently wipes out the line in the sand)

DAVID: I want to see what happens when a fucking wall comes down!

(Lights up on JAIME *being interviewed by the detectives.)*

JAIME: Jaime Fernandez. *¿Esto va tomar mucho tiempo?* ...Sorry, you don't understand—*es que mi familia*— my family is scared, they need me. ...No, I don't have anything against—*este gavacho cree que tengo aspecto de*—yes! You think I look like a killer, all my life I know that look! I am a family man! A businessman—I own five Tony Romas! ...Sorry, I am very angry about the Pope, he is one of us! *No merece*—he shouldn't die for Nuevo California. May I go to my family now?

(Lights up on ALBERT, *still in his bloodied shirt; he enters with* SIN FIN *closely behind.)*

SIN FIN: Mister Man of the Clan! *¡Soy Sin Fin la Parlanchin! Silencio* ain't my style, *dejame cantar lo que vi,* Sarah Lee. What I saw before the Pope got the call to fall.

ALBERT: For Christsake, I don't have time for this.

SIN FIN: *¡Pero escucha! I want to help find the sender of bullets de rencor, señor!*

ALBERT: Are you on drugs?

SIN FIN: No need to feed *la* stereotype!

ALBERT: Get out of my face!

SIN FIN: Oh, I *veo lo feo. El Papa's* fall you couldn't call.

ALBERT: Yes, I could. I did. I just couldn't stop it from happening.

SIN FIN: The cross is heavy and *duele mucho-rucho. Es* okay, Rey, spirits got your back.

(SIN FIN exits. DAVID sees ALBERT, approaches him.)

DAVID: Hey, We met last night. *(Beat)* That was very brave...what you did, protecting the Pope like that.

ALBERT: It was reckless.

DAVID: *(Re: ALBERT's bloodied shirt)* His blood?

ALBERT: *(More to himself)* I was less than ten feet away from him. God has deserted this planet, I swear it. *(Noticing JUANA)* Juana?

DAVID: Juana?

ALBERT: *(To JUANA, re: DAVID)* ¿Estan juntos?

(JUANA says nothing.)

ALBERT: Juana, *necesito hablar contigo.*

(DAVID takes a photograph of ALBERT.)

ALBERT: *(To JUANA)* No tienes que estar en esta fila si no quieres.

JUANA: *No quiero su ayuda.*

DAVID: It doesn't look like she wants to talk to you.

ALBERT: Fuck off.

DAVID: Like that's going to make the Pope any better?

(ALBERT decks DAVID with a single blow.)

JUANA: Albert!

ALBERT: Juana...*por favor. Ven conmigo.*

JUANA: No. *Me quedo con el gringo.*

DAVID: Gee, thanks.

ALBERT: Fine, stay with your *gringo*, and tell him about your little boy Sebastian.

JUANA: Albert, *porque?*

ALBERT: *(Pointedly to* JUANA*)* Because family is
everything. *No me he olvidado de tu hijo.* And I certainly
haven't forgotten about you.

DAVID: Where's her son?

ALBERT: Ask her. Maybe she'll also tell you what
intimate pleasure she had because of her negligence.

JUANA: *¡Sabes que...vete a la chingada!*

*(*JUANA *slaps* ALBERT *hard.)*

ALBERT: *Muy bien.* For my stupidity I deserve worse.

JUANA: *(Somewhat regretful) ¿A donde vas?*

ALBERT: *(Slight pause)* Where else? Church.

*(*ALBERT *exits.* DAVID *sits facing the detective/audience, as
does* JUANA *on another part of the stage.)*

DAVID: Detective, it says right there, I work for *Time*
magazine. Yes, I know it's an antique camera. ...Yes,
I was taking photos when it happened. ...Couple rolls.
I develop them in a dark room like a caveman. Here,
you can have them. ...You want my camera, too?
But my dad gave me—

JUANA: *Porque no quiero hablar ingles.* ...*¿Y a mi que me
importa si sus jefes no hablan español?*

DAVID: No, I have nothing against this Pope...but I
would ask the Vatican about Pope Pius II and Hitler.

JUANA: Okay, okay. I try English.

DAVID: Okay, okay, take the camera! But I want it back
in one piece.

JUANA: *Pero les digo una cosa*—I say one thing to you—
eso de abrir la frontera es ilusorio—to open the border is
fantasy—*por no decir imposible.*

DAVID: Let me tell you one thing—cynical as it might
sound—our world can't cope without borders.

JUANA: *Siempre ha sido*—always us in the south—trying to survive. While the north take advantage of us.

DAVID: What's important is who we are, not where we're from.

JUANA: Your country is eating us alive!

DAVID: I'm starving.

JUANA: Your country is a monster!

DAVID: A glass of water?

JUANA: *¿Yo? Personal motives?!*

DAVID: Wanna see me drop from exhaustion?

JUANA: I don't want to hurt *el Papa!*

DAVID: I didn't see anything!

JUANA: *¡No vi nada!*

(Lights out on DAVID *and* JUANA, *up on* REBECCA*)*

REBECCA: *(To camera/audience)* One hour since Pope Felipe slipped into a coma. The scene here at Las Playas is raw, harsh. Everywhere I look I feel the pain, horror, shock and terror. Raucous sea birds in great number circling overhead. *(Beat)* The Presidents of the United States and Mexico have finally arrived in Air Force One and are at the Pope's bedside. *(Beat)* And the old adage, "better late than never" rings in my ear. A bitter irony for all the world to see. But the late, great Sarah Vaughn said it best, "Send in the clowns." Two irresponsible governments have created a political climate which takes down the most innocent lamb.

(Lights up on a bed where FELIPE *lays unconscious. Sounds of monitoring devices. We see the shadows of the* PRESIDENTS *hovering over him; they speak quietly to each other.)*

PRESIDENT GOLD: You lost our bet, Señor Presidente.

PRESIDENTE CORTEZ: Did I, Madam President?

PRESIDENT GOLD: You said the Vatican would take him down before Christmas.

PRESIDENTE CORTEZ: Yes, and you said he would be stopped by a lone gunman in a fedora.

PRESIDENT GOLD: Poor man... Strange to see him silent like this.

PRESIDENTE CORTEZ: What a relief.

PRESIDENT GOLD: I'll say. He was once so loyal to the Vatican.

PRESIDENTE CORTEZ: Yes madam President, he was once one of us. If he dies...

PRESIDENT GOLD: ...he will become a formidable martyr.

PRESIDENTE CORTEZ: Remember, madam president, he was warned.

PRESIDENT GOLD: We have to move quickly President Cortez.

PRESIDENTE CORTEZ: Address our nations. By the way, I promise to give you the best prices on our crude oil.

PRESIDENT GOLD: *Gracias, amigo.*

PRESIDENTE CORTEZ: And in turn, I want your support with my political problems in Mexico City.

PRESIDENT GOLD: Naturally. We will stay high above this crime.

PRESIDENTE CORTEZ: Naturally. *¡Guardias!* And what do I owe you, dear friend?

PRESIDENTE GOLD: Your French chef for an entire year... and a fedora. May God protect Felipe's misguided soul.

(The two PRESIDENTS *make the sign of the cross with little reverence. Lights up on* SIN FIN *in a chair addressing the dectective/audience.)*

SIN FIN: *Por fin* someone who'll listen to Sin Fin! No, detective connective, Alex is what *mi amá* calls me, *ahora* my name is Sin Fin. I'm here to *contar lo que vi* on the sands of Playas. I'm *diciendo que* I am a witness to the big bang-bang, *soy testigo amigo!* *(Beat) Vi el Papa* get lead, felt it in *mi tripa, digo deepa.* And now *mi alma llora like flora.* ...*Lo que vi* and what I saw is this:

(A deconstructed version of the moment before the shooting begins. We see FELIPE *in the midst of giving his speech...)*

FELIPE: I know as I too have been excluded...

SIN FIN: And as *el Papa* spoke *con* his heart *abierto...*

FELIPE: I stand before this bit of rust...

SIN FIN: *Vi un glint en el sunray...*

FELIPE: I say it is forever possible ...

SIN FIN: *Un flash en mi cerebro...*

FELIPE: Let us not be afraid...

SIN FIN: *Un moment en cual el timeclock se paró...*

FELIPE: God's wondrous hand descends...

SIN FIN: *Si*yes, a glint.

FELIPE: Let the walls...

SIN FIN: A *pistola caracola!*

(Blackout on SIN FIN *and the scene she's just described. Lights up on* JUANA *on a lonely street.* DAVID *is suddenly there, a bag in his hands.)*

DAVID: You think I followed you?

JUANA: Crazy American.

DAVID: Oh, English now?

JUANA: *No. Esa frase es universal.*

DAVID: How was your interrogation? Your interview?

JUANA: *No me torturaron.*

DAVID: They wanted to torture me alright. *(Beat)*
Is this your house?

JUANA: *Si. Veo que no te quitaron la camera.*

DAVID: *(Indicating his camera)* The cops gave it back.

JUANA: *(Gesturing her meaning) ¿Porque tomas fotos?*

DAVID: Why do I take pictures? Call it a compulsion.

(Off her dubious look)

DAVID: Call me crazy—

JUANA: *Hola,* crazy.

DAVID: Pictures are evidence that we exist, that the
world matters. The camera lens, it's... *(Pointing to his
eye)* ...my eye. Photography is proof. Plain and simple.
Dumb, huh?

JUANA: *¿Tonto? ¿Tu? Si, un poco. (Smiles) ¿Y que mas
prueban?*

DAVID: *Prueban?*

JUANA: Proof.

DAVID: Oh. A photograph is tangible. Real. Yet, when I
shoot the Pope...something just jumps right through the
lens.

JUANA: *La presencia de Dios.*

DAVID: God? No, no, not God, give me something real
and tangible. Something I can touch.

JUANA: God is not something you can touch.

DAVID: Look, I'm sorry, I didn't come to argue.

JUANA: Then why?

DAVID: *(Holding up a roll of film)* I hid one roll in the
sand. The last one before the Pope was shot. Anyway,

a hotel room isn't safe. I thought I could develop it here.
I need a dark room. *Cuarto oscuro.* I trust you.

JUANA: *(Surprised)* Confias en mi?

DAVID: Yes or no?

JUANA: *Pasa.*

*(Lights change. Sounds of various monitoring devices.
FELIPE, barefoot, but still in his vestments, enters.)*

FELIPE: What is this place? *(He feels where his wound
should be.)* The bullet...? Heavenly Father, are you here?
Maybe I can find my way back...
Where is the way back? Where was it? Where was I?
*(Unsuccessfully finding any way out or back to where he
came from)* Dear Father. Not yet. I'm not—I have so
much to—please, please let me... Let me go back!
(He pounds his fists against the steel fence.) Let me be your
instrument! Let me live! *(He stops pounding, exhausted.)*
Please, dear God, don't leave me alone. Take away
this awful stench. *(Beat)* Please. Father. Hold my hand.
Take me to your love...take my hand...

VOICES: Felipe...Felipe...

FELIPE: *(Not fully aware of the voices)* Take my hand...

VOICES: Felipe...

FELIPE: Let go!

VOICES: Felipe!

FELIPE: Please let go! Let go of me!

*(Lights change to reveal three masked Dead Spirits, they are
the* CHORUS OF THE DEAD.*)*

FELIPE: Who are you?

CAMPESINA WOMAN: *Esmeralda Ponce. Soy de Oaxaca.
Mori en 1998 de un puñalazo cuando traté de cruzar la
frontera.*

FELIPE: Murdered at the border?

CHINESE WOMAN: I am Ping Chang, from Xiamen, China. I died in a storage container in the desert.

PERUVIAN MAN: I am Domingo Jaramillo, *de* Peru. I died crossing through a tunnel underneath the fence.

FELIPE: What?

PERUVIAN MAN: We died because of this fence.

CAMPESINA WOMAN: We are trapped here.

CHINESE WOMAN: You not dead.

FELIPE: *(Relieved for a brief moment)* Dear Christ! Dear Christ! *(Beat)* Not dead. Are you certain? How can you know such a thing?

CAMPESINA WOMAN: We know.

FELIPE: I feel so strange.

PERUVIAN MAN: Because you are not dead...yet...

CHINESE WOMAN: You can help us.

CAMPESINA WOMAN: *Liberanos.*

CHINESE WOMAN: Free us.

PERUVIAN MAN: Finish what you started.

CHINESE WOMAN: Before death comes.

PERUVIAN MAN: Take down this awful wall.

CAMPESINA WOMAN: Free us.

FELIPE: *(Wrestling with his disquietude in this new realm)* God loves you.

CAMPESINA WOMAN: Does he?!

CHINESE WOMAN: If you die...

PERUVIAN MAN: As we died...

CAMPESINA WOMAN: You will remain with us....

PERUVIAN MAN: In this region between light and cold,

CAMPESINA WOMAN: Far from heaven.

PERUVIAN MAN: Lost souls.

CAMPESINA WOMAN: *Por eternidad.*

FELIPE: God loves you, my children.

PERUVIAN MAN: As he loves you?

FELIPE: I have surely angered God....

CHINESE WOMAN: What did you expect?

FELIPE: I was plucked off the Earth before my time!

PERUVIAN MAN: Angry Felipe.

CAMPESINA WOMAN: You are here.

CHORUS OF THE DEAD: *You are.*

FELIPE: This is too much to bear.
Father. *Padre. Por favor, señor.* Answer me.
I deserve an answer!
These poor souls need your help.
I need your help.
Am I to stand before death alone?
Father, shine your light before my fear.
Muestrame tu luz divina.
Save me.
Take my hand, lead me from here.
(Silence)
Show me the glorious power of your love. Show me
your naked face. *(Silence)* Show me something! *(Beat)*
Nothing? *(Beat)* What do you want from me? Purge
my anger? Forgive the crime done against me?!
How, without your help?! How?! *(Beat)* Still nothing?
(Tearing off a portion of his vestment) Then I choose to
forget all that you've taught me. An eye for an eye!

CHORUS OF THE DEAD: A candle for a candle.

(Each of the CHORUS OF THE DEAD *intone the following in Spanish, English and Chinese—the jumbled whispering that* FELIPE *has been hearing throughout the play.)*

CHORUS OF THE DEAD: The people that walked in darkness have seen a great light.
They that dwell in the land of the shadow of death, upon them hath the light shined.

FELIPE: God of Silence! I reject you! *Ad infinitum!*
Not Pope Felipe anymore!
I'm free of you!
I'm falling!
Only a man!
I'm only a man!
Only a man!

*(*FELIPE's *vestments lie in pieces on the sand. The* BIRD *swoops down upon him, making the most amazing sound ever heard on this planet. Blackout)*

END OF ACT ONE

ACT TWO

(Lights up on FELIPE *and the* BIRD*)*

FELIPE: *(To* BIRD*)* Are you here to steal my breath?

*(*FELIPE *suddenly notices the* CHORUS OF THE DEAD *appear from the fence.)*

CAMPESINA WOMAN: Felipe, Take down the wall.

FELIPE: I want to see the face of God.

CAMPESINA WOMAN: But here we see only God's Eternal Shadow.

PERUVIAN MAN: Only the truly chosen see God's Magnificent Face.

FELIPE: Take me to see the face of God.

(They all get a whiff of FELIPE'*s stench and recoil.)*

CHINESE WOMAN: That smell?!

CAMPESINA WOMAN: Felipe's body was failing before the bullet hit. Maybe this is the stench of a future death.

PERUVIAN MAN: Maybe Satan played a joke and gave Felipe his intimate smell.

CAMPESINA WOMAN: And you've taken in...

PERUVIAN MAN: ...what was rancid among every nation and race in this world.

CAMPESINA WOMAN: Charm...

PERUVIAN MAN: And prayer...

CAMPESINA WOMAN: Are not enough...

CHINESE WOMAN: For God to show you his true face.

CAMPESINA WOMAN: But first you have a difficult task.

PERUVIAN MAN: *Hombre.*

CAMPESINA WOMAN: *Pobrecito.*

CHINESE WOMAN: *Jiaohuang.*

FELIPE: A task?

PERUVIAN MAN: Yes. For millions of people...

CHINESE WOMAN: You must be a channel for the injured who have lost a loved one.

CAMPESINA WOMAN: You must become the loved one.

CHINESE WOMAN: You must prepare each person for change.

PERUVIAN MAN: Before the sun rises.

CAMPESINA WOMAN: Before the sand sets and you join us forever within this wall.

(The BIRD *lets loose a horrifying scream, cutting into* FELIPE's *core)*

FELIPE: *(Beat)* How do I do this?

PERUVIAN MAN: Close your eyes.

*(*FELIPE *complies; the* CHORUS OF THE DEAD *shroud him with a cloak.)*

FELIPE: I'll be someone who died...

CHINESE WOMAN: Yes.

PERUVIAN MAN: You'll meet thousands of loved ones every minute. Rich and poor alike.

CAMPESINA WOMAN: On and on and on until everyone is accommodated.

CHINESE WOMAN: And shitty odor is gone.

FELIPE: I will live the memories of a million dead?

CAMPESINA WOMAN: And you will begin to take down the wall.

PERUVIAN MAN: In exchange, we can help you find what you seek.

FELIPE: I seek my God.

CHORUS OF THE DEAD: Come with us.

(FELIPE exits with the CHORUS OF THE DEAD. The beach fills with New Cal Supporters carrying candles, effigies and posters of FELIPE. They continue chanting and adding to the altar for FELIPE. REBECCA is there as well.)

NEW CAL SUPPORTERS: *Dios protega a*
Nuestro Padre Felipe,
Santo y nuestro guia espiritual.
God protect Holy Father Felipe,
Saint and spiritual guide.

REBECCA: Rowland here at water's edge. There is a mood of muted disbelief . A sorrowful crowd building a makeshift shrine. Hear the sincere tears of a sad people. *(Beat)* His Eminence—very near death. Presidents Gold and Cortez have condemned the heinous shooting. Lawyers work around the clock to save this virgin City-State. And to quote *The New York Times*, "If the Berlin Wall could come down, certainly freedom should flourish in our own Pacific backyard."

(Lights up on SIN FIN before the detective/audience)

SIN FIN: Okay-dokey, inspective detective, but before I can pick up slack, gotta start further back.

(As she speaks, we see the deconstructed version of what she describes.)

SIN FIN: It's yesterday, before Felipe's speech beseach... I see*veo* the ocean*mar* and I want to offer my dream*sueños* to the *espiritus* of *la* nature, to *lanzar* my body into the water and *purificarme* of all things that prevent me from being a spirit of light and truth, but there's more: I see*veo* the memoria of all presente... I see*veo* some with hurt *en sus* eyes from too much blaming shaming defaming. And others *con sus ojos* full of fear of the bet. *Pero otros con* eyes ablaze, *con ojos* full of rage, and all of a sudden I see*veo*...I see*veo*...I see*veo*...

(We see the figure of a man in a long coat, his face completely obscured by a hat)

SIN FIN: A man standing still.

(Lights up on DAVID and JUANA looking at the photos he's just developed.)

JUANA: *No veo nada raro. Solo gente y mas gente.*

DAVID: Yeah, nothing strange there except a streak of light.

JUANA: *Espiritu de los muertos.*

DAVID: Huh?

JUANA: Ghosts.

DAVID: *(Uncomfortable laugh)* Look, um...*gracias.* For letting me work here.

JUANA: Y esto?

DAVID: Uh...photos...of you. I...saw you in the crowd. *(Beat)* What happened to your son?

(JUANA tries to ignore DAVID's question.)

JUANA: *(Re: the photo in her hand) Mirela, con esperanza reflejada en sus ojos.*

DAVID: Come on, I know you speak some English.

JUANA: *Y yo se que tu hablas un poco de Español.*

DAVID: Okay, I'll try if you try. *Yo trato* also.

JUANA: I said.... *(Indicating the photo)* She has so much hope in her eyes.

DAVID: I thought she looked like you. *Parece* like you.

JUANA: *Y tu*, who do you look like?

DAVID: People used to say *mi padre*.

JUANA: *Antes dijiste*—you are Jewish?

DAVID: *(Pronouncing like* JUANA*)* "Jewish?" Yeah, *mas o menos. (Beat)* Until one day—*un dia*—I was given a test.

JUANA: *Otra prueba?*

DAVID: Jews are fond of tests. Moses was a wiz. *(Beat) Dos años* ago *mis padres* went back to the Holy Land. For...*la vida*. With all the other settlers who've been fighting—*peleando*—with Palestinians over a strip of land. So I went to visit them. *Visitar.* My father insisted we all go see Jerusalem. So we're on our way to the Wailing Wall—a glorious wall—when we encounter some Palestinians. Suddenly everybody's quoting all the prophets Jesus, Mohammed, Whoopie Goldberg! So my dad and this Palestinian blow up! *Muy bravos. Mi madre* barely gets us out of there and back into our jeep. *Mi padre*, still pissed off, turns around to make another Zionistic point about a Holy Land, but he never gets past the first words because he runs a red light. Plows into a truck. He's dead. *Muerto. Mi madre* also. All in an instant.

JUANA: *Lo siento.*

DAVID: So. I failed the test. So did Spinoza, Einstein, Phillip Roth-in their own brilliant ways all failed the Jewish people. Because they couldn't meet impossible expectations. No matter how caring they were. Maybe they weren't Kosher enough. *(Beat)* So I'm not interested in being a normal Jew if you see me by way of your preconceptions. *No soy Judio mas.* I'm just an inane man with an heirloom camera. Anyway, whose *tierra* is *mas sagrado*? I mean, what is sacred? Is it your birthright to claim priority over someone else's birthright?

JUANA: I don't know anymore.

DAVID: If everyone is so concerned about sovereignty and culture and pissing rights—seems logical to ask what's so *importante* about a place?! What's so great about this one?!

JUANA: *Es aqui donde nacimos.* It's our home.

DAVID: Well, mi padre wasn't born in the Holy Land, but he called it his home and it became his goddamn grave. If he weren't such a zealot, if he hadn't been fixated on some utopia in his imagination—

JUANA: *Su imaginacion no los mato!* A truck killed them.

DAVID: That doesn't stop me from thinking about their death every day. *(Beat)* I'm not going to make the same mistake. *(Beat)* Maybe I will. Maybe I will.

(Pause)

JUANA: I wanted to be a doctor. I was studying in the university...*me enamore. (With some disdain)* Love. I became....

DAVID: Pregnant?

JUANA: We married. My son was born. *Adios* career.

DAVID: You gave up your dreams to have a child?

JUANA: My husband Ramon...was an engineer. He built the energy plant for Albert.

DAVID: *(Getting a much fuller picture)* I see.

JUANA: *Pero nunca estaba en casa*, Ramon never home. Albert knew it hurt me. He gave Ramon even more to do at the plant. *La planta que es tan importante a Nuevo California.*

DAVID: And your son?

JUANA: Sebastian? Sebastian... *(With difficulty)* ...*era mi compás.*

DAVID: What happened to your husband, Juana? What happened to Sebastian?

(DAVID gently touches JUANA's hand; she yanks it away.)

JUANA: *No. No te voy a contar.*

DAVID: You're not going to tell me?

JUANA: *No. Eres de alla. Eres mi enemigo.* You are from the other side.

DAVID: I'm not your enemy.

JUANA: Are you sure?

(JUANA exits. Lights reveal FELIPE and the PERUVIAN MAN entering. DAVID doesn't see FELIPE or the PERUVIAN MAN.)

FELIPE: Why is he among the first? *(Re: DAVID)* Does he know who shot me?

PERUVIAN MAN: Put this on.

(PERUVIAN MAN holds out a yarmulke)

FELIPE: That is the cap of a dead Jewish man.

PERUVIAN MAN: *Si.* And now your task begins.

(PERUVIAN MAN places the yarmulke on FELIPE's head, causing a sudden and powerful transformation, the first of many in which FELIPE embodies both himself and a dead loved one. FELIPE now recognizes DAVID.)

FELIPE: His name is David. My son.

DAVID: Dad? *(Beat)* This can't be.

FELIPE: David. It is me. At least I think it is.

DAVID: It's a dream.

FELIPE: So is birth. Death. And everything in between.

DAVID: Fuck, it's you all right.

FELIPE: David...who shot the Pope?

DAVID: I was there, Dad. It was horrible.

FELIPE: What did you see?

DAVID: Just what was in the lens of my...your camera.

FELIPE: Then you saw shit.

DAVID: Why did you come back?

FELIPE: You stupid—I was plucked off this earth before my time! I had unfinished business!

DAVID: My business ended with you when you flipped out in Jerusalem! Buying all that religious crap killed you and Mom!

FELIPE: But, David, I had plans, dreams, many years left in me!

DAVID: Goddamnit, you plowed into a fucking truck!

FELIPE: Okay! I screwed up.

DAVID: I said Kaddish for you to mourn your soul. Eleven months of prayer.

FELIPE: I know you did. *(Tender silence)* So now I have to praise you. What's important is *mitzvoth,* good deeds, good actions.

DAVID: Judaism makes no sense to me.

FELIPE: That is the essence of our religion.

DAVID: I hate you.

FELIPE: Don't say that.

DAVID: You abandoned me.

FELIPE: You're right. Absolutely right.

DAVID: I won't let you haunt me.

FELIPE: David I'm so tired of my anger. I want my soul to be at peace.

DAVID: You look good pissed off.

FELIPE: Anger is the key to my charisma.

DAVID: Your anger was the key to getting you killed.

FELIPE: Who needs charisma. *(Beat)* My son. Teach me.

DAVID: *(Incredulous)* Teach you?

FELIPE: Yes. I must listen to you.

DAVID: And we'll make up for lost time?

FELIPE: You reflect my true face.

DAVID: Dad...have you...?

FELIPE: I walk through sand colder than ice. *(Beat)* Goodbye, son. I have to hurry.

DAVID: Why?

FELIPE: *(Realizing)* I have people to see.

DAVID: Dad! I love you.

*(*FELIPE *embraces* DAVID, *then exits. A moment later,* JUANA *enters, sees* DAVID's *state.)*

JUANA: David? *Que pasó?* Are you okay?

DAVID: I saw my father, He was here.

JUANA: A ghost?

DAVID: No, no, no, ghost, he was here, it was real.

JUANA: *No tomaste foto? Como prueba—*

DAVID: No photo, I saw him. *(Beat)* You think I'm lying?

JUANA: No I don't. *(Beat)* David I need something to show you. Come. *Ven.*

(JUANA *leads* DAVID *off. Lights up on Playas.* REBECCA *is on-air.*)

REBECCA: There are literally thousands of reports from area residents saying they've been visited by ghostly apparitions of dead lovers and relatives. What can I say dear friends? Is it tequila? Or "to kill ya?" I've just talked with Cardinal O'Brian from Chicago who said that many Vatican officials were eager to discredit the Pope, at the expense of humiliating all Catholic institutions. He went on to say that Mexico is "not quite a geography, certainly not a mature, civil nation. And Nuevo California is simply a decorative ribbon sitting atop forty million beautiful barrels of Kumeyaay Reservation oil a day." *(Flip)* Brilliant analysis, Cardinal O'Brian! Bravo! *(To camera/audience)* This just in. I B C has received exclusive footage taken by an East Lake resident:

(*A* UNIFIED PATROL OFFICER *shines her flashlight on a* SUBURBAN MAN *who is trying to erect a fence of his own.*)

U P O: Sir, I'm with Unified Patrol. There've been complaints

S M: This is my property, and I've every right to build a fence.

U P O: Sir, it's three A M.

S M: I should use the one you idiots threw away. My neighbors are meeting in secret. They say the Pope was shot to send a message. And now it's time to tell the whole world that Nuevo California must die.

U P O: Give me the shovel.

S M: NO!

U P O: Give me the shovel.

S M: Get off, this is my shovel! Go back to where you came from!

U P O: Give me the shovel.

S M: My shovel!

(The U P O *unsuccessfully attempts to take the shovel.
The* S M *beats her savagely with the shovel)*

S M: My house! Mine! Mine! Mine! Shit, turn that
camera off!

(Back to REBECCA*)*

REBECCA: *(To camera/audience)* The officer died on the
scene. *(Improvising)* The perpetrator mentioned secret
meetings being held. *(Beat)* I know in my bones that the
Pope's shooting was not the act of a single "madman".
I can also name the people who have inspired this
unspeakable act. It's only a matter of time before
everyone is unmasked. This is Rebecca Rowland in
Nuevo California.

(Lights up on FELIPE *and the* CAMPESINA WOMAN.*)*

FELIPE: These visits to the living are comforting.
A gentle voice inside my head calms me.
Where has my rage gone?

CAMPESINA WOMAN: You are listening to other angels
now.

FELIPE: Yet I'm no closer to God. Has Christ abandoned
me?

CAMPESINA WOMAN: It is a very dark night.

*(*FELIPE *begins digging a circle around himself, addressing
the sand, the sea, the stars)*

FELIPE: Cizin! My Mayan ancest.r, god of earthquakes!
Are you here? *(Beat)* Cizin. I carry your blood. Come.
Guide me. *(Facing each direction he describes)* The East,
Yellow Road, source of life. The West, Black Road,
place of darkness. The North, White Road, place of
the divine. The South, Red Road, path of—

(The BIRD *enters.)*

FELIPE: *(To* BIRD*)* Has Cizin sent you?

(The two circle each other, evolving into a dance of intimacy. It is suddenly broken by the sound of medical monitoring devices, FELIPE *falls to ground in agony as his earthly body fails him)*

FELIPE: I hear the machines fixed to my shriveling body. *(To* BIRD*)* I give you my heart...give me time.

CAMPESINA WOMAN: But dawn will not wait. Felipe. The wall.

FELIPE: I can't go on!

CAMPESINA WOMAN: You are afraid like the boy you once were. *(Tenderly)* Your heart opens each second like a morning flower. Come...come...

(The CAMPESINA WOMAN *and* FELIPE *exit. Lights up on* SIN FIN *before the detective/audience.)*

SIN FIN: Detective collective...I remember *mas* from yesterday. *Dejame* paint the details *con* these words... *(Her vision continues...)* I see*veo* the man standing still. Standing still like a drill, ready to kill, *me siento* so ill, no can make a picturerama. ...Sorry*siento, siento*sorry

(Suddenly we aware of JUANA *now standing next to the Man Standing Still)*

SIN FIN: *Pero* wait! The man *esta rapando* with a señorita, a frown pointed down *con trizteza* like a contessa of doom and gloom, and she talks to him *con certeza* and she smiles a secret smile. *(Calling out to the detective)* Wait, detective, I didn't say she—don't go, bro, not without Sin Fin!

*(*SIN FIN *runs off. Lights up on Playas as* MAGGIE *and* JAIME *enter;* MAGGIE *carries a U S flag,* JAIME *a Mexican one.)*

MAGGIE: We're not here to criticize or complain
We just think the status quo should remain

JAIME: *La barda es muy importante para nosotros*
Para mantener alguna distancia de los otros

REBECCA: *(To camera/audience)* The vast show of military
might in front of me is sickening. Where were these
soldiers yesterday? Rumors of the Pope's death has
only added fuel to this civil hell.

MAGGIE:	JAIME:
Hello and goodbye...	*Este plaga tiene que ir*
Nuevo California	*Nuevo California*
Must die.	*Debe morir.*

REBECCA: An hour ago in El Paso a gang of kids
murdered an old trucker who had a confederate flag
in his front cab. The kids were shouting Rowland,
Rowland, Rowland. I find this quite disturbing.

MAGGIE:	JAIME:
In full voice we cry	*Para que mentir*
Nuevo California	*Nuevo California*
Must die	*Debe morir*

(MAGGIE commandeers REBECCA's microphone, speaks to
the camera/audience.)

MAGGIE: I want to tell you a story. My family owned
an avocado ranch in Fallbrook. We employed Mexicans,
people I'd known for years. People I loved. We let them
live on our ranch. They were celebrating Mexican
Independence Day. They got drunk and let their bonfire
get out of control. Burned down their camp...and my
home, the house my great-great-grandfather built.
And these "friends" that I trusted...they just sat there
and laughed. Good fences make good neighbors!

JAIME: Let me tell you a story.

(REBECCA allows JAIME time with the microphone as well)

JAIME: My brother has a daughter, sixteen years old, an angel, a gift from God. One night after a dance at Casa de Cultura in Tijuana, a drunk U S marine promised her the moon. We found her six hours later. Beaten. Raped. *(Beat)* My niece will never dance again. You dance with Uncle Sam, you dance with the devil!

MAGGIE: *(To* JAIME *and his camp)* Go back to where you came from!

JAIME: Go back to where *you* came from, pilgrim!

*(*ALBERT *runs on, addresses the crowd/audience.)*

ALBERT: Listen to me! We've a great opportunity to build paradise! Build the best schools and hospitals!

JAIME: Nuevo California is obscene, amigos!

ALBERT: We can build beauty in this land!

MAGGIE: Nuevo California is...

JAIME: Worse than a concentration camp!

MAGGIE: You call this freedom? Nuevo California is not....

JAIME: Liberty!

ALBERT: Open your goddamn hearts!

JAIME: Nuevo California is facism! Nuevo California is....

MAGGIE: ...bastard hybrid Spanglish fills the very air we breath!

*(*FELIPE *enters and try as he might, no one hears him)*

FELIPE: Albert, don't!

ALBERT: Listen to me!

MAGGIE: Here he is, ladies and gentleman, Mr Albert Venado! *(Pointing at him)* Is this the kind of demon you want to see making decisions in your name?

JAIME: A whore who trades his own people for oil and personal power!

ALBERT: Bullshit!

MAGGIE: The power plant that he's so proud of? Drilling oil over his ancestors' burial grounds!

JAIME: Sacred ground!

MAGGIE: His utilities company finances New Cal.

JAIME: I'll piss on his grave.

MAGGIE: This clown doesn't know whether he's Mexican,

JAIME: Indian,

MAGGIE: ...or J D Rockefeller.

ALBERT: You're twisting the truth, morons!

JAIME: This man sees money, not people.

ALBERT: Shut up!

MAGGIE: Let's not forget the drowning death last year of a little boy...

JAIME: Here on this beach!

ALBERT: *(Losing the composure he has left)* You cocksuckers!

JAIME: It was his negligence that led to that boy's death!

MAGGIE: But you didn't hear about it, because his political pals covered it up!

ALBERT: I've brought prosperity here, you dumb fucks! My heart...

JAIME: Pinche coward!

MAGGIE: Killer of innocent children!

ALBERT: *(Experiencing sudden chest pain)* There was no goddamn cover up!

MAGGIE: *(Now directly to* ALBERT*)* Get out of my sight, you make me sick.

JAIME: *(Directly to* ALBERT*)* Asesino!

ALBERT: My heart! *(Bends over trying to catch his breath)*

MAGGIE: That's right. Go fuck yourself!

JAIME: Monster! Have a heart attack!

FELIPE: Stop this obscene behavior! The man is my friend!

MAGGIE: Go away, you filthy beast!

*(*MAGGIE *and* JAIME *hurl rocks at* ALBERT, *chasing him off.)*

REBECCA: "It is no vicious blot nor other foulness, no enchase action, or dishonored step, that hath depriv'd us of out grace and favor" ...from Shakespeare's *Lear.* "Now gods stand up to bastards!" *(Beat)* God help us all.

(Lights up on DAVID *and* JUANA *as they enter a remote section of the beach)*

DAVID: Why did you bring me here?

JUANA: Sebastian. My son...he died here. *Es como...* I feel Sebastian still. Calling to me. Every day.

DAVID: What happened here?

JUANA: *Mi hijo,* he was fascinated with the United States. Everything good, *todas las maravillas,* were over there. That's all Sebastian talked about. *Que iba hacer esto, iba visitar a tal lugar,* Hollywood, Washington, Memphis—

DAVID: Memphis?

JUANA: *Por Elvis Presley. Tenia ocho anos y hablaba mejor...*his English perfect.

DAVID: You never considered moving to the States?

JUANA: *Soy Mexicana.* No, to Ramon I said no, *nadie en mi familia* is going to live in *gringo*landia.

DAVID: Juana...what happened here at the beach?

JUANA: Sebastian loved to come, to show me where the fence ends in the ocean, *y me preguntaba*, "Mama, is the water different over there?" He wanted to know what it taste like on the other side. *(Beat) Un dia*, Albert came with us. Sebastian took off his shoes, "Mami, hold my shoes". Then he walked into the water along the wall. Albert and I made a mistake. We kissed. We went too far. *(Silence)* "*Mami, mami*" *(Beat)* Sebastian was in trouble. He was swimming and swimming and trying to go around the fence to the other side, but, he was caught in a, *como se dice corriente*—

DAVID: Caught in a riptide?

JUANA: Swallowing him *como un monstruo. Iba a devorarme tambien*—I wanted the monster to swallow me too, *queria estar con mi hijo*, but Albert grabbed me, *gritandome que me moriria tambien*. Sebastian disappeared. *(Beat) Para siempre.* Forever.

DAVID: I'm so sorry.

JUANA: Ramon blamed me for Sebastian's death. *Y se fue.* I lost a husband and a son. *(Beat)* Now you know why I hate the United States.

DAVID: Yeah.

JUANA: And why I hate myself even more.

DAVID: Juana.

JUANA: I lost his shoes in the water. *(Beat) Es como* his memory is here in my mind. *Y encima de todo...* His love, was so real. Not imagined, but real. I feel him every time I come here. His tears on my face, *saben al mar*, like the sea. His delicate hands pulling mine. I feel him, here.

(ALBERT enters, he's been looking for JUANA.)

JUANA: *Albert, que paso?*

DAVID: What's going on?

ALBERT: *(To* JUANA*)* The police are coming for you.
I have to hide her. *Hay un testigo que dice que estabas junto a un sospechoso.*

JUANA: *No es posible.*

DAVID: Somebody?

ALBERT: A witness puts her next to the assassin.
(To JUANA*)* Creen que lo conoces.

JUANA: *Pero como—?*

ALBERT: Do you know the man who shot Felipe?

JUANA: *Vete.*

ALBERT: I won't let them touch you.

JUANA: *Ya, Albert. Vete!*

DAVID: She wants you to leave.

ALBERT: *(Sincere tone to* DAVID*)* Please. Only I can protect her now.

JUANA: *No voy a colaborar con la policia. De ningun país.*

(Sound of approaching sirens)

JUANA: *La policia.*

*(*JUANA *runs off.* DAVID *goes after her.)*

DAVID: Juana, wait!

*(*ALBERT *is left alone. He recognizes this spot of the beach, begins digging underneath a specific mound of rocks. A moment later,* FELIPE *enters, not yet seeing* ALBERT*)*

FELIPE: I need to rest. I'm so tired.

*(*FELIPE's *earthly condition is worsening. The* BIRD *appears)*

FELIPE: You wait to swoop down and feed from my carcass. My body is rotting, yet to me I smell like a sweet garden of roses.

(The BIRD *gestures gently.)*

FELIPE: Was it you who saved me in the desert? Were you my boyhood hallucination? I don't have much time left.

(The CHINESE WOMAN *from the* CHORUS OF THE DEAD *enters)*

CHINESE WOMAN: Felipe

*(*FELIPE *notices* ALBERT *as he unearths a little box; out of it he pulls out a pair of small shoes.)*

FELIPE: What does Alberto need?

CHINESE WOMAN: The same as you.

FELIPE: To take down a wall.

(The CHINESE WOMAN *wraps a shawl around* FELIPE *who now transforms again, but this time into...)*

ALBERT: Grandmother? Abuela, why are you here? We burned all your belongings, your memories are free to go with you.

FELIPE: You must've missed something. *(Indicating the shoes in* ALBERT'*s hands)* What do you have there, Albertito?

ALBERT: Shoes.

FELIPE: The shoes of a child. Oh, no. No, no, no, these don't belong to you.

ALBERT: They belonged to Juana's son. I found his shoes. I didn't steal them.

FELIPE: Light the flames that will set his memories free. It is our way.

ALBERT: I know, grandmother.

FELIPE: No, you don't.

(The BIRD *makes a large, expansive gesture.)*

FELIPE: *(More as* FELIPE*)* Alberto...the story...the monster who terrorized the Kumeyaay children?

ALBERT: *Si, abuela.*

FELIPE: There was a boy, wasn't there?

ALBERT: *Si.* He killed the beast.

FELIPE: What did the beast look like?

ALBERT: It was a bird.

FELIPE: *Ah, si, Albertito,* I remember now. A great bird that we brought upon ourselves. *(More as himself)* I should've known. We negotiate with the bird. *Quid pro quo. (Indirectly to the* BIRD*)* Your life for my life. Your soul for my soul. *(Back to being grandmother)* Do you remember how the boy killed the bird?

ALBERT: He let the bird chase him into the river where the current was strongest. And the boy grabbed the bird by its talons, then dragged the bird down under the water with him, and—

FELIPE: And together they died. The boy knew he would have to die to save the children.

ALBERT: Is that part in the song?

FELIPE: *(Completely as himself)* It should be.

ALBERT: Felipe?

FELIPE: *(Covering)* Eh...who, me?

ALBERT: Abuela, you really had me going, for a second there I thought you were Felipe.

FELIPE: Hmm.

ALBERT: I love him so much. I'm so afraid.

(FELIPE *embraces* ALBERT.)

FELIPE: The boy was afraid. But what matters is that his
sacrifice...his sacrifice gives meaning to others.

(FELIPE *sees the* BIRD *fly off, he exits after it.* ALBERT *looks
at the shoes, his decision made. Lights up on* JUANA, *now
before the detective/audience once again.*)

JUANA: *No, no tengo nada que decir a la policia!* English,
English. I tell you already, I have nothing to say.
Not to police. ...I can wait too. I wait a hundred years.
A thousand! (*As if watching detective leave room*) *¡Si, hasta
que el mundo se acabe!*

(SIN FIN *enters*)

JUANA: *Usted quien es?*

SIN FIN: Sin Fin. Sayer of prayer. *Voz veloz. La que* put
you here, *la que* can help put you into the clear.

JUANA: *Como?*

SIN FIN: *Señorita dinamita*, no one's *diciendo que* you're
the *asesina.*

JUANA: *No quiero hablar con la policia.*

SIN FIN: Deep down they want *lo que* you want.

JUANA: (*Challenging*) *¿Y que es lo que yo quiero?*

SIN FIN: You want a place *en tu* heart *que es libre*, free
of pain the reign of broken glass *y* fear of losing *lo* little
que is left of life—giving forgiving. I see*veo* your pain *y
mucho* more in your core. I see*veo* you drowning in a sea
of guilt.

(*Pause*)

JUANA: (*Indicating* SIN FIN, *for benefit of detectives
listening in*) Okay. (*Pause*) I will talk to her.

SIN FIN: *Oy vey*, okay I say. (*Beat*) I see*veo* you with a
man of stone.

JUANA: *Si.*

SIN FIN: Do you know him?

JUANA: No.

SIN FIN: What did he say yesterday?

JUANA: *Nada.* I spoke to him. I was angry at seeing the people-why should they be happy...*¿y yo no?* I shared my poison with him...like you do with a stranger. *Le dije que* the United States kills our hopes, *nuestros sueños*...our children. *(Pause)* My words. *Mis pensamientos*...they caused him to shoot. *Si. Yo soy culpable.* It's my fault!

SIN FIN: No.

JUANA: *¡Si!*

SIN FIN: Your words didn't fire the bullet.

JUANA: *¿Y porque no?!*

SIN FIN: Everyday...I seeveo the looks of those who fear tomorrow. And yesterday...all those gentepeople took a breath of fear sin light. And he...he squeezed the bullet with all our fright. *(Realizing) No hay un* jail big enough for all of us who flinch at *mañana*day. *(To detectives)* So, please...arrest us all!

(Playas. Lights up on FELIPE*)*

FELIPE: Dear God...I have seen so many faces. I have walked in the moment of their pain. Everywhere so many walls falling. *(Beat)* Darkness is lifting.

(The BIRD *appears before him.)*

FELIPE: You could take me right now. Why are you waiting?

(Lights up on ALBERT, *who has dug a pit and started a small fire in it. He begins to sing a Kumeyaay song as he places Sebastian's shoes in the fire. This has an immediate effect on*

FELIPE, *who regains some strength. The* CHINESE WOMAN *from the* CHORUS OF THE DEAD *enters, removes the shoes from the fire and approaches* FELIPE *with them.)*

CHINESE WOMAN: If you choose to kiss the face before you, rose petals will rise into sky.

FELIPE: We die again and again, don't we?

CHINESE WOMAN: Yes, but for the last time if you succeed. I have faith in you.

FELIPE: This is my final step, isn't it? My final death. One more. *(He notices his shaking hands.)* My hands shake with fear. No clothes? Only shoes?

CHINESE WOMAN: Only shoes.

*(*FELIPE *holds the shoes in his hands. Lights reveal* JUANA—*just released*—*standing on the beach alone. She looks up and sees...)*

JUANA: *¿Sebastian? (Beat) ¿Sebastian?*

FELIPE: *Mami.*

JUANA: *¿Entonces...estas vivo?*

FELIPE: No, *mami*...I'm not alive.

JUANA: *Tus zapatos.*

FELIPE: Yes, I have my shoes. ...*Mami, Mami*, I'm so afraid of what's ahead. Hold me.

JUANA: *¿Pero ne ves? (She touches his heart, does everything she describes.) Tu corazon...lo estoy abrazando...aqui en el mio. Y mi corazon...esta con el tuyo tambien.*

FELIPE: My heart with yours? Forever?

JUANA: *Para siempere.*

FELIPE: Why are you crying, *mami?*

JUANA: *Los Estados Unidos te mataron.* They killed you.

FELIPE: But *mami*, I've seen the other side of the ocean.

JUANA: *¿Y que vista alla?*

FELIPE: It was the same there. *Lo mismo.* Don't hate the americans, *mami.*

(He touches her heart, doing the same as she did to him a moment ago)

FELIPE: They are here. And here too. Don't you feel them mami? Tumbala. No more walls. Especially ones you make yourself. *Tumbala, mami...tumbala.*

(ALBERT finishes singing the Kumeyaay song. The shoes are burned and are only ashes now. Lights fade on ALBERT as...)

FELIPE: *(More as himself)* Help us accept the sting of death. Help us all. Liberanos.

JUANA: *Si, mi hijo. Si. Si.*

(FELIPE embraces JUANA.)

FELIPE: Gracias, Mami. We are now free to take the next step.

(FELIPE exits. The BIRD exits behind him. After a moment, DAVID enters.)

DAVID: Thank God I found you. *(Sensing a change in her) ¿Juana, que paso?*

JUANA: *Mi hijo...*I saw my son. *(Beat)* Do you think I'm crazy?

DAVID: No.

(DAVID throws his camera into the ocean)

JUANA: *Tu camera, tu prueba.*

DAVID: The proof I need is not in that camera.

(After a moment, she gently kisses him. He gently kisses her back. They exit. FELIPE enters with the CAMPESINA WOMAN.)

FELIPE: I have relinquished my anger.
Conquered my fear of tomorrow.
I am ready....

CAMPESINA WOMAN: You are a very handsome soul
this morning.

FELIPE: Will Nuevo California survive?

CAMPESINA WOMAN: If led by those who lead not from
fear...

FELIPE: There are still two thousand miles of it at
Mexico's feet.

CAMPESINA WOMAN: Some fences so long and wide.
But you do what you can...

FELIPE: One step at a time. *(He holds a handful of sand,
lets it slip through his fingers.)* So beautiful.

(Lights up on SIN FIN *before the ocean.)*

SIN FIN: *Viento lento,* akin to *el papa's palabras. Por favor,*
allow me to *seeveo mas alla,* through the pale veil of *cosas
misteriosas.* Give me sight, *mirada consagrada...*

(The BIRD *appears, allowing itself to be seen by* SIN FIN.)

SIN FIN: *Ave que sabe.* Bird of knowing, vision glowing.
Show me. *Muestrame.* Show me, *Ave.*

(The BIRD *begins to lift its wings and reveals a figure....)*

SIN FIN: I see*veo...el* man standing still...is you.

*(*SIN FIN *is able to communicate with the* MAN STANDING
STILL—*the moment before he shoots* FELIPE, *cutting across
time and space.)*

M S S: What do you want?

SIN FIN: *Es usted,* zed.

FELIPE: *(Re: m.s.s.)* I smell rancid blood. My blood.

*(*FELIPE *also now is able to see the* M S S.)*

SIN FIN: You're about to shoot the lovely lovely lovely Pope.

M S S: You don't see it? He's changing everything.

FELIPE: Is change so frightening?

M S S: *(To* FELIPE*)* It's you?! How can that be?!

FELIPE: Because it can. Is it fright that you fear?

M S S: You make us question everything! Up is way down, evil is so good...they're me and...I could be them.

SIN FIN: *Quien es* "them"?

M S S: American Mexican Catholic White Black Muslim Buddhist Gay Straight Albino Brown Yellow Red Hindu Protestant Methodist Mason Theosophic Athiest Everyone!

FELIPE: And you?

M S S: One singular fantastic! One of all who dares to be one of one!

SIN FIN: What do you mean, dean?

M S S: I want order in the universe!

FELIPE: What is order?

M S S: When every animal knows its rightful place!

SIN FIN: Your *mundo confundo* I understand *con* scarity clarity!

M S S: Everything about you offends me!

(M S S points his gun at SIN FIN, *severing her connection to the scene.* FELIPE *recognizes that* M S S *is about to snap.)*

FELIPE: I know of the need to control what should be. But maybe there are things we shouldn't have knowledge of. Maybe the wind never knows its destination.

M S S: You demand change! I hate change. And I failed.

FELIPE: You are a messenger who has delivered his message. How is that failure?

M S S: You stand before me. Didn't I kill your soul?

FELIPE: No, but...you stole my arrogance. "Of unblemished life and spotless record". How arrogant of me to want perfection. *(Beat)* Forgive me for my arrogance.

M S S: For your tolerance?! For what you allow?! For your destruction of order?! Just fucking die!

(The M S S points his gun at FELIPE*; it's as if he's going to shoot him all over again. The* BIRD *screams and the* M S S*'s arm withers, lays limp at his side.)*

FELIPE: Take my hand. I forgive you your trespasses.

*(*FELIPE *embraces the* M S S*, who reacts as if he's being embraced by death itself.)*

M S S: No, no, no, no...

(The M S S *pulls away from* FELIPE *and slowly backs offstage. We hear a single gunshot. Pause.* FELIPE *sighs deeply.)*

FELIPE: My mind is clear.
My heart is clear.
My soul is clear.
(To the BIRD*)*
Come for a swim with me?

(The BIRD *gestures a kind of acquiescence and they disrobe an outer layer of clothes.)*

FELIPE: There's nothing to be afraid of, dear one.

*(*FELIPE *leads the* BIRD *into the sea, both gradually disappearing under the waves.)*

(The masks of the CHORUS OF THE DEAD *are released.)*

(We become aware of many people standing on the beach near the fence. It's as if they all sense that something incredible has happened-negative or positive no one can say)

REBECCA: Ladies and gentlemen...Pope Felipe has passed away. It appears he felt no pain. The world as we know it will never be the same.

(SIN FIN steps forward.)

SIN FIN: *Ahora mi corazon llora*
And my heart bleeds
A life has left and *eso causa una pausa*...
I pause and pray today
To find a place in my heart
Donde a grudge can budge
Donde puedo perdonar and forgive and let live
To see beyond a line in the sand
Un muro that won't let me see *el futuro*
A fence that screams *y acusa offence*

I need to know who *es el otro.*
Es tu my friend,
And me and everyone I see?
Is the other the guy with who I lie in bed?
My mother in a different dress no less?
Mi papa que da y da y gives me his blood in a flood?

I want to take my fear *y mirarla* clear
No se todo que viene mañana day
But I want to take the leap
To where it's deep
And *tomar el paso hacia* tomorrow

Time to look to the *futuro*
Does it have to be *tan duro?*
If you agree my sister and my brother
Let's take a step and then another

(SIN FIN, with great effort, tears off a piece of the fence and throws it onto the sand. Then another, and another, each time

making a thunderous noise of steel against steel. Exhilarated and exhausted, she stops for a moment.)

REBECCA: It's *(Date)*. I'm Rebecca Rowland. This is Nuevo California.

END OF PLAY